PERSKE
PENCIL PORTRAITS
1971–1990

Perske Books from Abingdon Press

Show Me No Mercy
Don't Stop the Music
Hope for the Families
New Life in the Neighborhood
Circles of Friends
Unequal Justice?
Deadly Innocence?

PENCIL PORTRAITS
1971–1990

Drawings by Martha Perske

Introduction by Robert Perske

Abingdon Press
Nashville

PERSKE PENCIL PORTRAITS: 1971–1990

ISBN 0-687-05080-4

98 99 00 01 02 03 04 05 06 07 — 10 9 8 7 6 5 4 3 2 1
MANUFACTURED IN SINGAPORE

For our kids
Ann, Dawn, Lee, Marc, and Richard

Contents

Introduction
On Trying to Understand Martha

Robert Perske

How can I explain a mystery like Martha Perske?

For three decades I have watched this self-taught illustrator draw faces of persons with disabilities—one after another. They appeared in more books, films, brochures, newspapers, magazines, and government reports than anyone can count. In each drawing, Martha struggled to give wings to anyone trying to turn his or her tough situation into a rich human experience. She worked hard, always trying to show a person's disability and natural beauty—both at the same time. She produced each face with a pencil—that's right, just a *pencil*.

Her focus was tiny but powerful, and she refused to move very far from it. Once I watched and chuckled to myself as an editor begged Martha to draw a landscape. Instantly, her usually quiet, kind mouth tightened up like a coin purse. Her eyes flashed a *never* that didn't need to be spoken. She made it plain that *she chose to do faces*—first, faces of persons with disabilities alone; later, mixed in with so-called "normals."

Although I have worked and slept with this mystery since 1969, I cannot talk Martha out of something she is determined to do. What's more, often there is no understanding of why she chose to do something until she reveals the reasons in her own good time and in her own way. What she shares often makes me want to hug her and hold her tight.

We met in Topeka when she was the single mom of Dawn, Lee, and Marc. She worked as secretary to the principal at Stout Elementary School, and later, for the assistant principal of Topeka High, her alma mater. I was the single dad of Richard and Ann, a fellow in religion and psychiatry at The Menninger Foundation and a chaplain at Kansas Neurological Institute. Our courtship amounted to something just a little less than a fistfight. By the time we finally decided to get married, our children were getting along better than we were.

After we married, I often came home and talked —too much, I thought—about what went on with my "parishioners" at KNI during the day. Martha always listened with interest. Then one day, she began to draw their faces.

The earliest drawings were signed only using her first name, MARTHA—an early indication to me and our friends that the durability of the marriage was questionable. At that time, I traveled with teams who described new principles being applied to persons with disabilities. We spoke with gusto about these "breakthroughs," as if each one were a Holy Grail in itself. One day I overpreached to

Martha about "The Scandinavian Principle of Normalization"—why our home should be "a normalized environment."

Then I saw the tightening coin purse, and that lovely five-foot-two body stiffened until she looked like a toy soldier. She marched around the house saying, "We must make this home normal!" (march, march) "We must all be normal in this house!" (march, march) "How is this for normal?" (march, march) "I will not be normalized!" (march, march) "You must accept me as I am!"

I got that message and pondered it for quite awhile! One day Martha began to affix PERSKE to her art with a flourish. Our thriving emotional and professional partnership became better each year.

Her first published drawings appeared in 1971 on covers of the *GOARC Gazette,* the newsletter of the Greater Omaha Arc. During that time, I sold my first manuscript and asked the publisher to consider backup art by Martha. The response was an emphatic, "No. I've been burnt too many times by husband-wife teams." But when he saw samples of her art he changed his mind.

After this success, Martha began to rehearse her gift with a vengeance, often working on a single face for days on end. Her workplace was a drawing board in a corner of the living room. It was a setting for eyestrain and backaches, and the large wastebasket overflowed with rejected drawings and wooden pencil shavings.

Her hard work netted awards from organizations throughout the world—but she refused to travel any great distances to receive them. (She once suffered a frightening experience on an airplane: It took off.) When they were awarded nearby, she did appear, but never gave an acceptance speech. What the audience got was a sincere, warm smile and a soft "Thank you."

She even received a request to present an autographed drawing to Her Royal Highness, Diana, the Princess of Wales. Martha prepared the drawing, a montage of six children's happy, upturned faces—some with disabilities and some without. But she refused to travel to the presentation. Her husband served as delivery boy. The drawing was presented in a special ceremony in Liverpool on September 20, 1989.

Although Martha is known internationally for her work, few people have ever met her. And yet, almost everybody within a ten-block radius of our home knows her well for something else. To them, Martha is that perky woman who every morning is seen being pulled through the town by her two little dogs, Molly and Jake, who move vigorously on a mission to say "hello" to every living creature they meet.

Being married to Martha has always been filled with uncertainties, but one thing is sure: Life with this woman has never been boring.

Martha's long days and nights at the drawing board have ended. The eyestrain and the backaches and the filling of the large wastebasket with rejected drawings and pencil shavings are no more. Now new projects take her time, and there's no asking her why. That answer will come only when she is good and ready to give it.

What drove her to work so long and so hard? Lots of hunches were voiced, but none were acceptable to Martha. After almost twenty years, she wrote an essay that hinted at what had been driving her. She did it for the kids and me. What she wrote follows in its entirety.

Memories of My Father

Martha Perske

The first memory I have of my father, Stafford Packard, was the night he had his stroke. He was thirty-two and I was five years old. I watched the medics come to our upstairs apartment with the stretcher and take him away. We were living in Kansas City at the house of my Grandmother and Grandfather Harding, my mother's parents. It must have been about 5:00 or 6:00 in the morning, because it was dark outside and I was sitting on the floor, looking at the funnies in the Sunday morning paper: a five-year-old's attempt to escape from a frightening reality—trying to concentrate on the funnies as her daddy was being carried away.

The next memory I have is sitting on the front porch of the Harding house, in a swing with my mother and father, probably six months to a year after his stroke. It was the kind of old-fashioned front porch swing that held several people, suspended by chains bracketed in the ceiling. It was a summer night, and the three of us were swinging gently in silence when I heard an utterance from my father's lips. It was indiscernible and I pretended not to hear it. But he repeated it, and this time I heard what sounded like "Marta." My father had been unable to speak since his stroke, and I knew that this was a momentous occasion

and that he had planned it as such—so that the first word I would hear him say was my own name, Martha. We were not a demonstrative family, so there were no shouts of victory. Rather, I remember simple, genuine smiles of happiness shared among the three of us. I went to bed happy that night—and proud.

The struggles that Mary and Stafford Packard went through during his recuperation period are not in my memory. I suspect I was protected from "adult concerns."

We continued to dwell in the upstairs of the Harding house. During this time Mary went to work and Stafford continued to recuperate, now being able to walk and talk. His right side was permanently paralyzed, and his speech sounded as if he had a German accent, a little hard to understand except for those of us close to him. All his life I remained "Marta."

I must have been about eight years old when we moved to Topeka. My mother, Mary, had found a good-paying job with the U.S. government. We lived with an aunt until we moved into a house at 1229 High Street. Mary had managed to keep us going financially. Stafford was still unable to work.

The house on High Street had two bedrooms,

and I was fortunate enough to get the upstairs sleeping room. This was to be my private domain throughout my school years.

Soon after we moved into this house, Grandmother Harding came to live with us. She was a widow by then. I figured she came to help keep the family going, since Mary was absent much of the time because of her job. We had no car and went everywhere by bus.

I was in third grade at that time, and found myself enrolled in an upper-class school called Randolph Elementary School. Most of my third-grade year was spent "getting sick" at school and having to go home, where I knew my daddy was. I don't remember exactly how I got from school to home on those "sick" days, but I think I walked. They weren't as strict in those days about letting kids leave school. I only remember entering our house, pulling out my coloring books, and lying on the front-room floor, happy with my books and crayons.

On one of those sick days, I remember that when my teacher helped me on with my coat so that I could be excused from the painful class-room she said, "Why do you want to go home?"

I replied, "Because my father is there, and he teases me and makes me laugh and feel better."

Her kind reply was, "Well, if you stay with us, we'll tease you, too, if it will make you feel better."

I somehow survived the third grade and pre-tended to myself and everyone else that, yes, I had adjusted to Randolph School. But I never really did, and those were painful years. I was different. My daddy was "crippled" (a term used in those days), and my mother had to work and could not visit school as the other mothers did.

There were other adjustments going on in our house, too. Stafford was a proud, independent soul, determined to survive his incapacitating stroke all by himself. One day while Grandma Harding was serving breakfast, he said he was going to get another bowl of cereal. Service-oriented person that she was, she said she would get it for him. He said no, he would get it himself. When she continued to insist, he flung his empty bowl to the floor in anger. This was a frightening experience for me. My parents had always been quiet, soft-spoken people. I didn't understand at the time his desperate fight to be independent and self-sufficient. No one was going to wait on him!

During those years leading up to Stafford's recovery, a steady, gradual honing took place. He learned to control his temper, and only to those closest to him was it obvious when his anger rose. The telltale sign that I knew so well was an inadvertent rising of his paralyzed right arm. I always knew when he was angry because that arm, which usually hung limp and lifeless at his side, would involuntarily rise to his waist. Those must have been humiliating times for him, because he would quickly grasp the arm with his good left hand, trying to prevent that telltale sign of rising anger.

He succeeded in conquering his temper and continued to progress. In my teenage years, however, I was to cause that arm to rise quite a few times.

My father was not one to be beaten. He learned to do everything all over again. Having once been right-handed, he learned to write all over again with his left hand. His speech became understandable, although those who didn't know him well still thought he spoke with a German accent.

He learned to walk again with the limp of one who has suffered a stroke.

And, I suppose that because he had time on his hands—and my mother didn't—he and I became bonded together by seemingly insignificant things. For instance, he had time to read the want ads and find a puppy for sale. Then he had time to walk the six blocks with me to where the puppy was for sale—Woodward Street. One of my vivid recollections is of our walking to get the puppy (I learned to walk slowly) and walking back home again with a tiny furry creature in my arms. It was the nicest gift my father could have given me, and I named her Toddles.

Even my Grandma Harding, who always smelled like soap and kept our house immaculate, succumbed to the charms of Toddles. Every year, she baked Toddles a cake with a candle on it for her birthday. And she herself saw to it that the dog was seated at the table as we cut the cake and sang "Happy Birthday"!

Stafford learned how to bake. He made the best lemon meringue pie I ever tasted. He could bake things with his left hand that most people couldn't with ten hands. His specialty was a jelly roll. He made everything from "scratch."

During my elementary school years, as my father was perfecting his lemon meringue pies, I continued to search for my mother. She traveled quite a bit for court cases that took her to places like Wichita and Chicago. On one of those trips I decided to go with her. I filled a brown paper sack with clean underwear and several pairs of socks, boarded the bus to downtown Topeka, walked several blocks to the Post Office, took the elevator up to the third floor, where she worked for the U.S.

District Court, and presented myself, paper sack and all, announcing that I was going with her to Wichita. Somehow I was returned home, and my mother went without me.

When I was in junior high school, my father landed a good job with the State, in the Motor Vehicle Department. But before that, I remember seeing him in his den, a room that was built onto the house especially for him. It was a small room, about the size of a walk-in closet, and I can see him yet, sitting before a drafting board with his ruler, patiently doing his work. Planning, always planning . . . something.

I remember the smell of chemicals from his darkroom in the basement, where he spent many hours developing film and enlarging photographs. To this day, I love the smell of a darkroom, and the memory of the soft red light in the dark basement.

I now see that these were the things that kept him going during those difficult years of rehabilitation—when his wife was the wage earner and he was incapacitated, but always possessing the spirit of a survivor . . . forever taking pictures . . . forever mapping out plans at his drawing board.

Unconsciously ingrained in me were those years of his determination, his persistence, his patience. He told me once that there was no such word as *can't*. When I doubted him, he got the dictionary and showed me. Sure enough, the word wasn't there. I believe it's there now, but thank goodness it wasn't there during my father's time.

He continued to work in the Motor Vehicle Department until his disability retirement. His stroke left him susceptible to pneumonia, and I remember one day when a car pulled up in front of our house and two people from his office helped

Martha with her mother and father.

house every morning at 7:30, my father at the steering wheel, picking up my classmates and dropping us off at Topeka High School. He would then deliver my mother to her office and proceed to his own job.

It was after my high-school years that he accepted a disability retirement from his job, due to recurring bouts with pneumonia. In between the bouts, however, I watched him sow a garden in his back yard that produced the biggest, sweetest strawberries you ever saw. And I saw that same proud spirit serving those strawberries, sprinkled with powdered sugar—that same proud spirit that had spent so many hours in the darkroom and at the drafting board—the spirit of determination that had enabled him to learn to drive a stick shift car with only one hand and one foot.

my father up the sidewalk to the house. He was sick, and this was the beginning of many hospital stays. Even so, he always returned to his job and was known as one of the most reliable persons in the department. He was slow, but he was deliberate. He was always accurate.

As I entered my high-school years, our family was able at last to purchase a car—a Ford. It was an occasion to celebrate. We took pictures and all took turns standing by the car—the camera recording this special event in our lives.

This enabled me to become part of a carpool in my high-school years (the 1950s). My father learned how to drive this mechanical wonder with only his left hand and left foot. I guess you might say he was more amazing than the car. We left the

Following his retirement, his health steadily deteriorated. A nurse was employed during the day in our house. There were frequent trips to the hospital. During his last stay in the hospital, my mother informed me that she had found a nursing home for him. I was in my early twenties at the time. The only time I ever saw my father cry was when he was taken to the nursing home.

Stafford died a year later, in 1963. He was taken again to the hospital where he had been so many times before. He was fifty-four years old. As word spread through the hospital that he was dying, all the nurses began slipping quietly into his room to say goodbye to him. Soon his bed was surrounded by nurses who had been his friends over the years. They smiled and spoke briefly with him. Some of them took turns holding his hand. My father's eyes twinkled and his handsome smile held no hint of sadness.

He once told me he wasn't afraid to die because then he would know what God was. That was one of the rare occasions when he spoke of a religious faith. And yet, at another time, when I was about sixteen and watched him as he tied his shoes with his left hand, I sensed that his quiet religion served as a driving force for him.

As I look back, I know that I learned a lot from my father. It was nothing he really tried to teach me. It was nothing he ever said in words. I learned just by watching him. Probably the most important thing he taught me was determination. He taught me to be on time, to be honest. I learned kindness because he was kind. He taught me the health-giving value of projects. And I learned that it is important to finish what you start.

October 10, 1989

PERSKE
PENCIL PORTRAITS
1971–1990

Martha '11

Martha

PERSKE

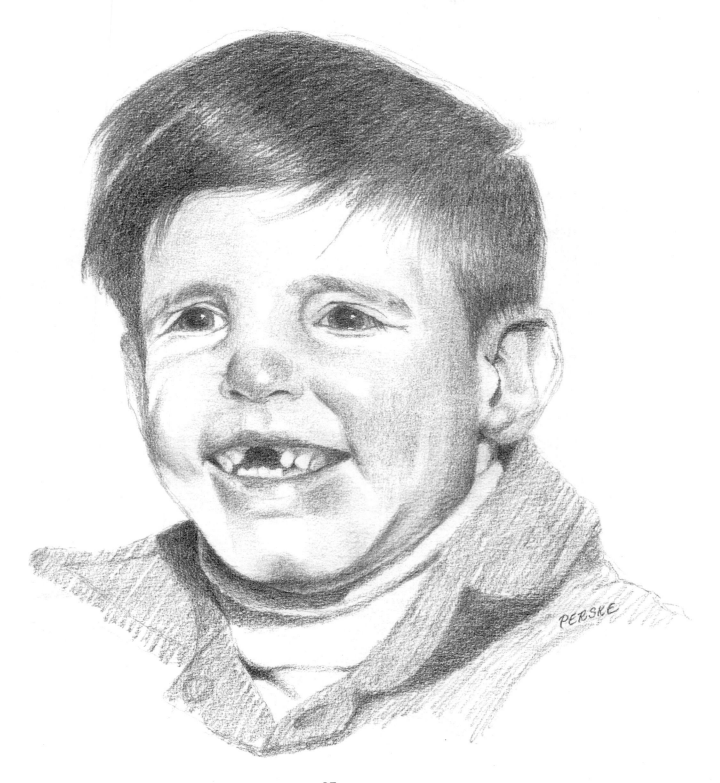

PERSKE

PERSKE

PERSKE

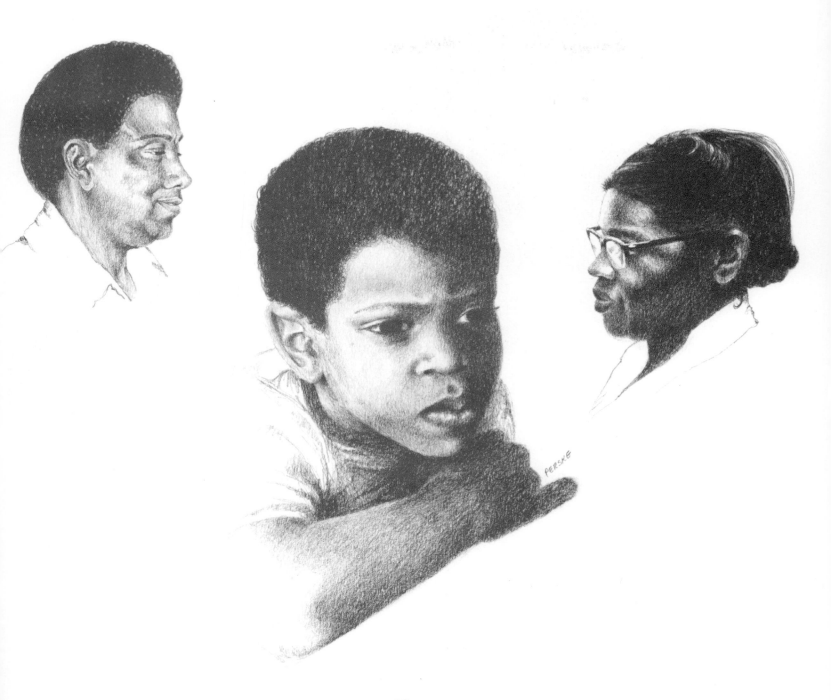

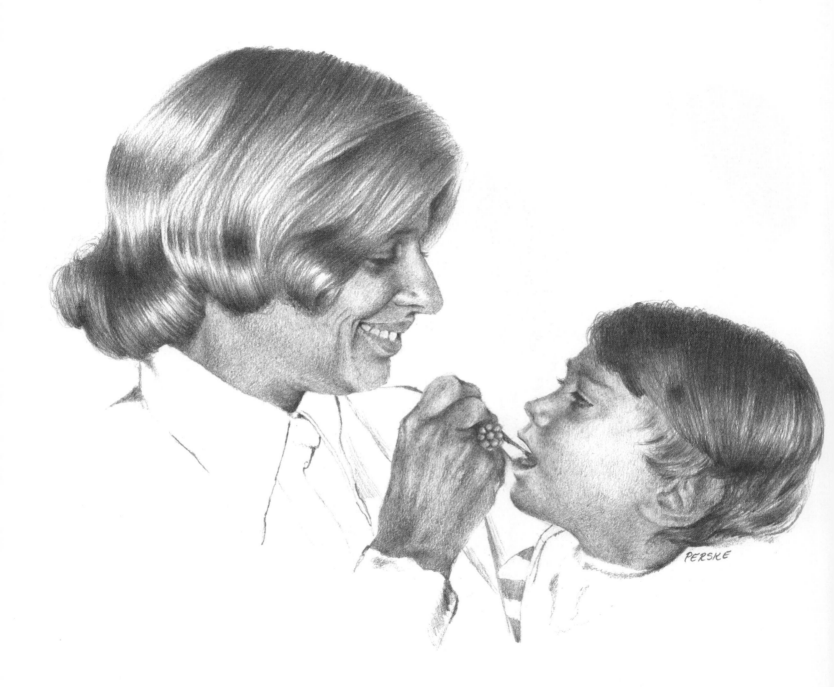

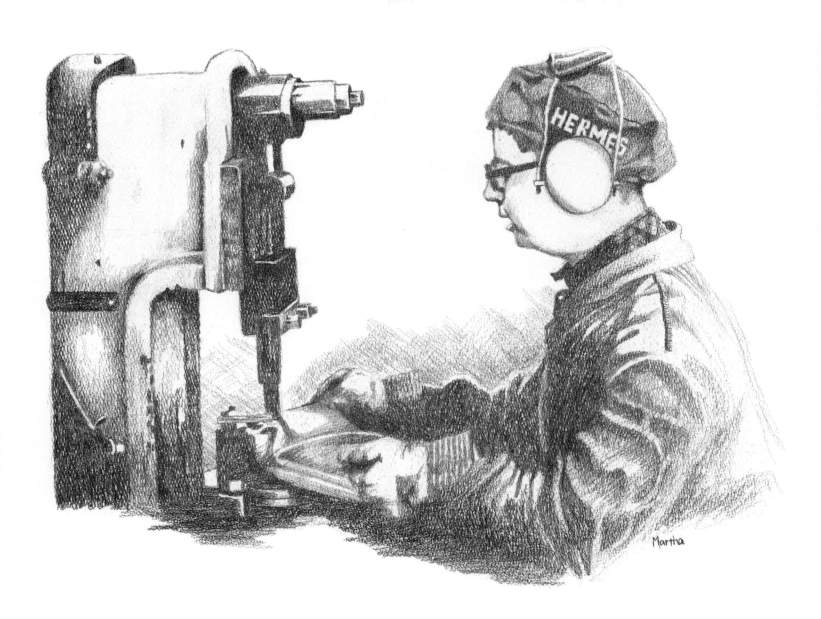

PERSKE

PERSKE

PERSKE

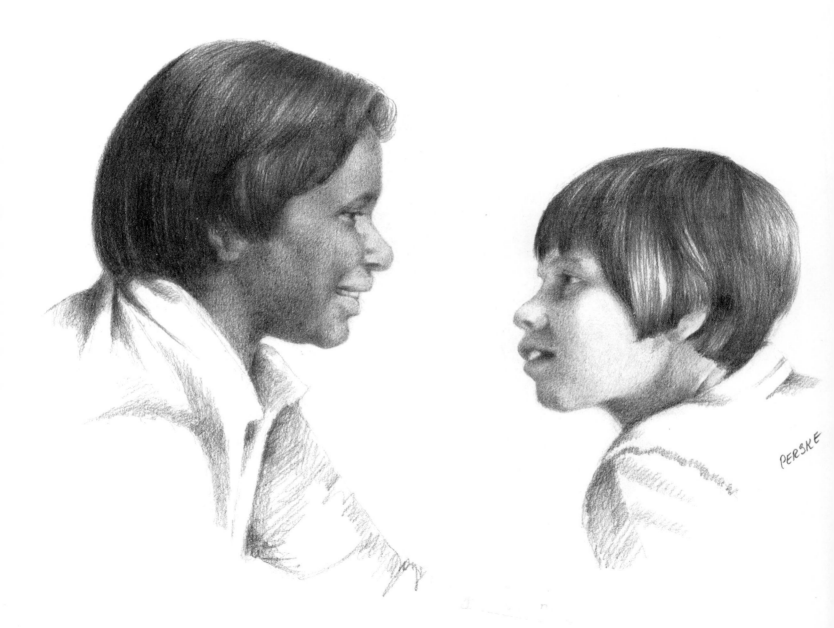

PERSKE

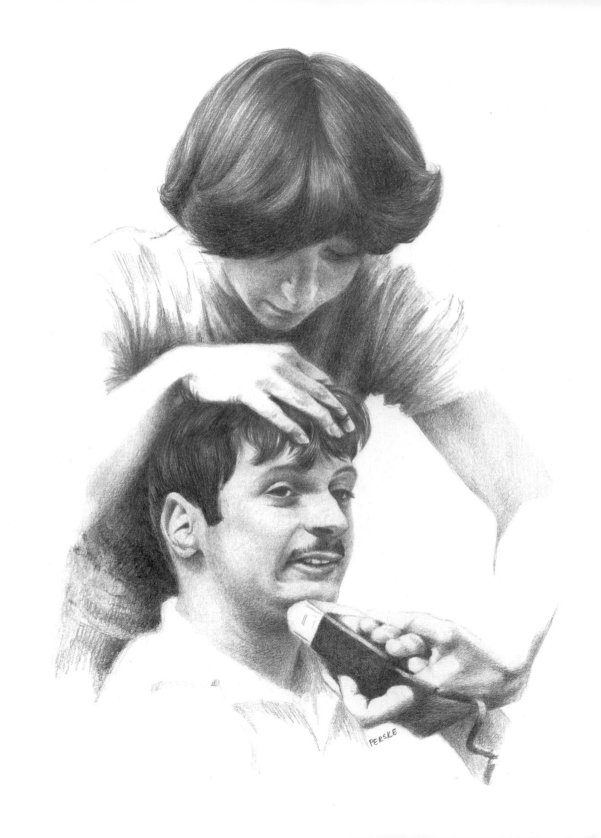

PERSICE

PERSKE

PERSKE

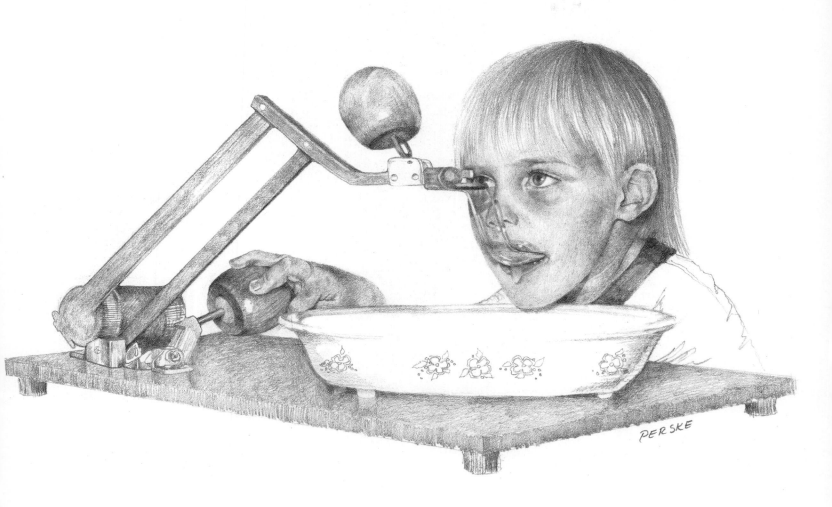

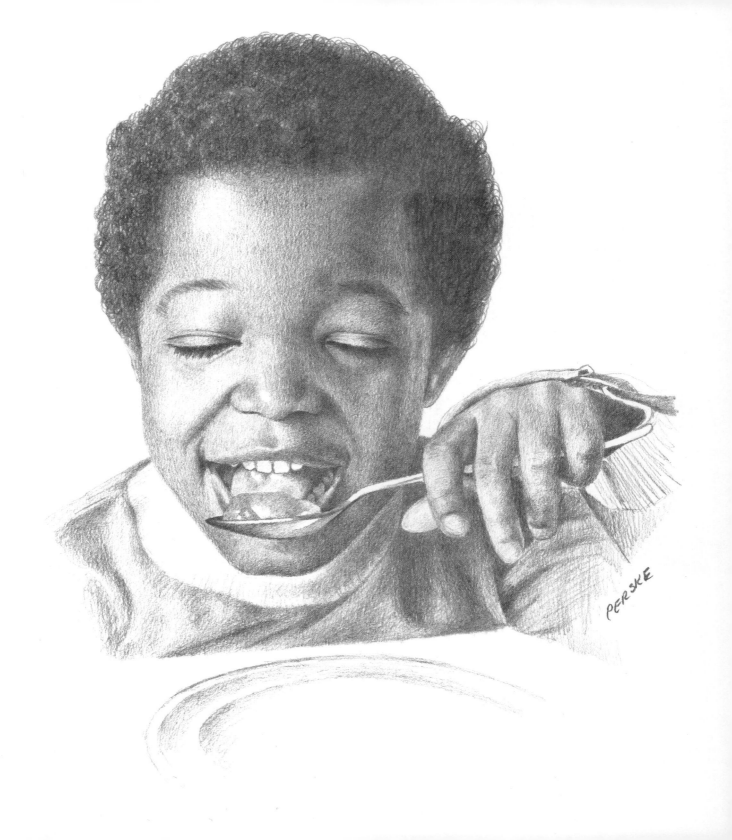

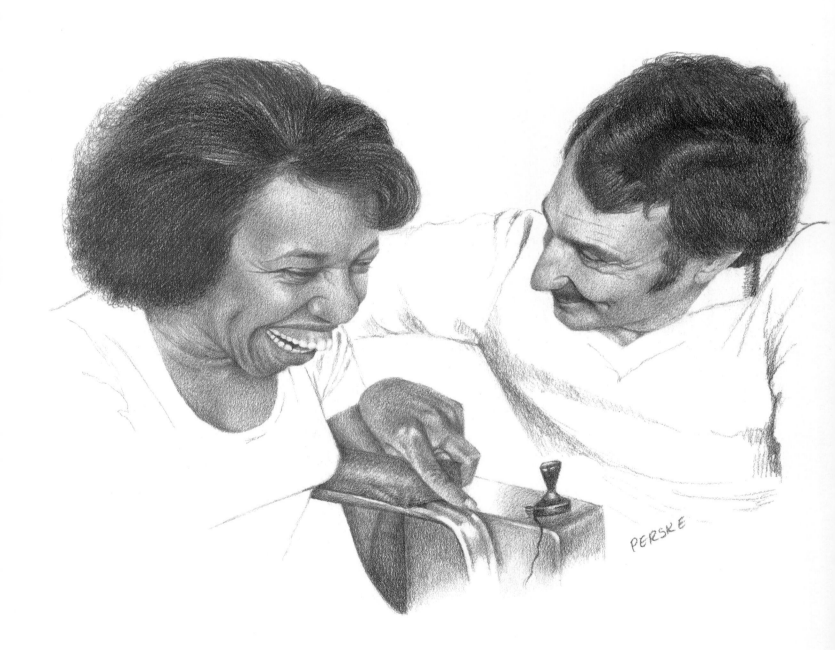

PERSKE

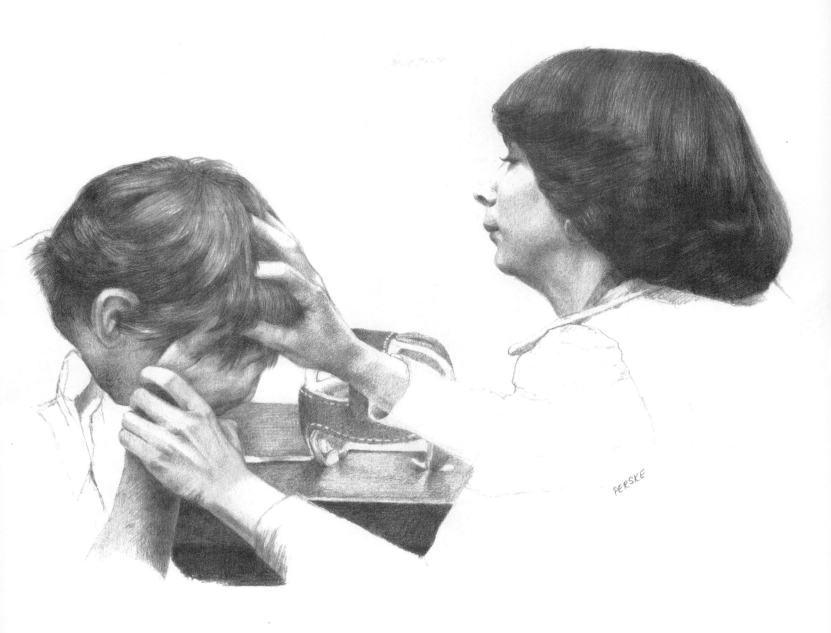

PERSKE

PERSKE

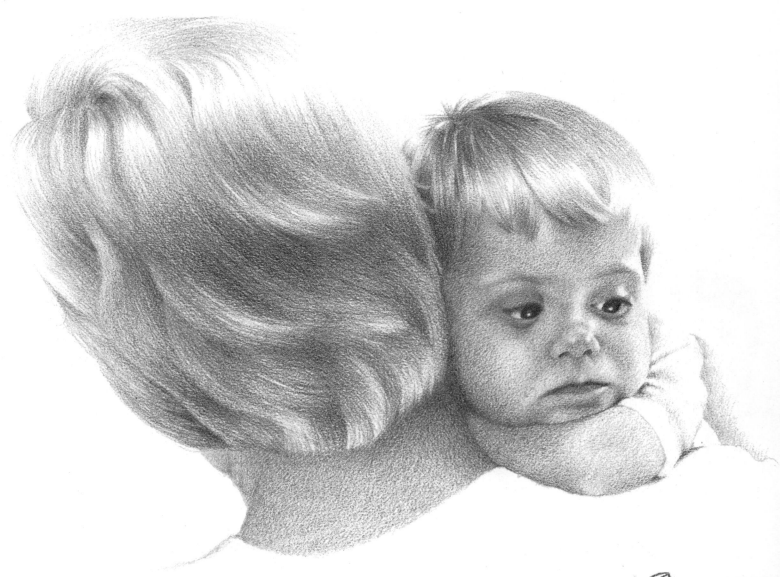

PERSKE

PERSKE

PERSKE

PERSKE

PERSKE

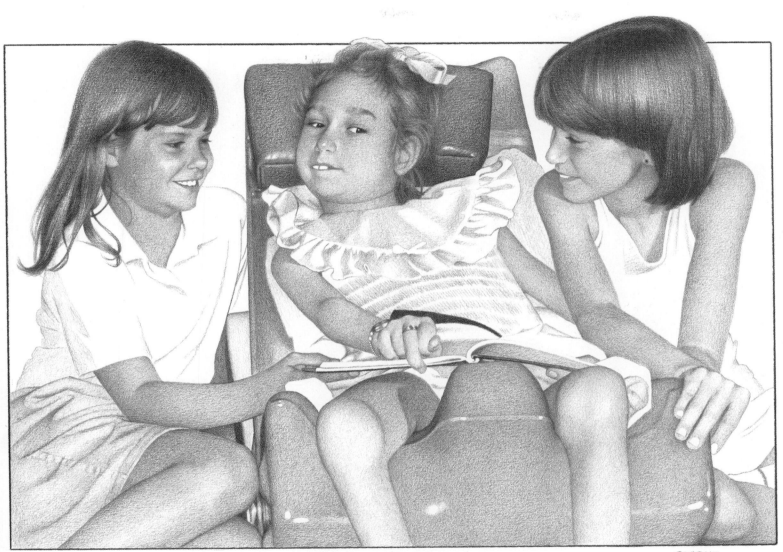

PERSKE

PERSKE

PERSKE

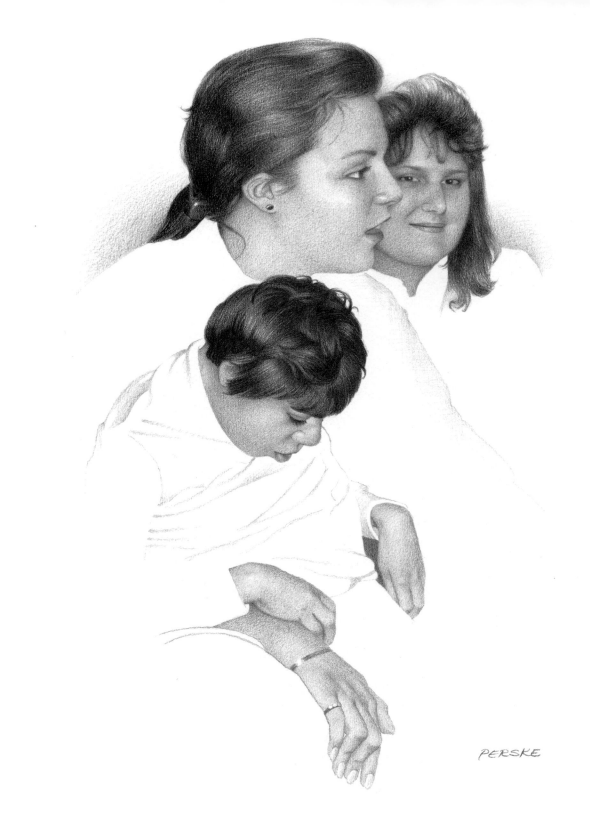

PERSKE

PERSKE

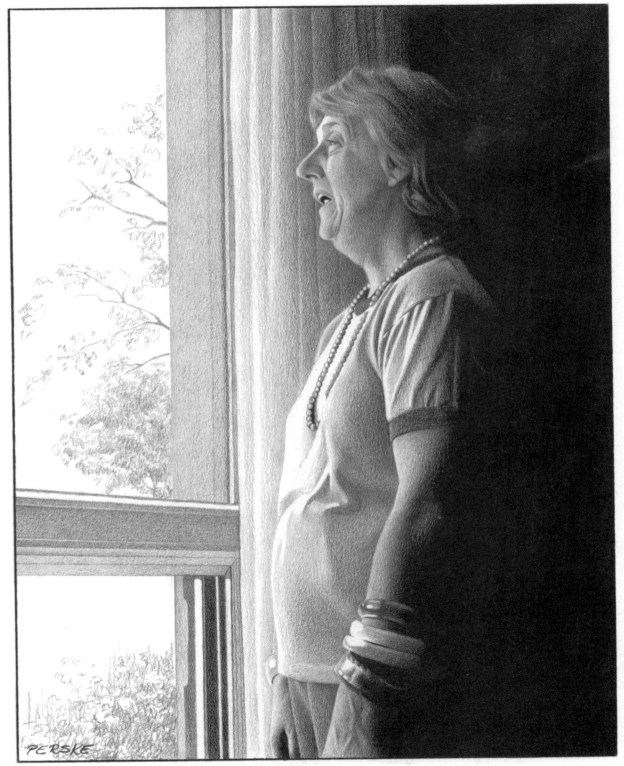

PERSKE

PERSKE

Most of the artwork in this book
was inspired by my husband,
Bob, who helped me to see
that we are all just guests on this earth.